5.62

MW01141658

Mystery history of a
PIRATE GALLEON

written by Fred Finney
illustrated by Mike Bell, Richard Berridge, and Roger Hutchins

O. L
Sherwo

COPPER BEECH BOOKS
BROOKFIELD, CONNECTICUT

© Aladdin Books Ltd 1996
Designed and produced by
Aladdin Books Ltd
28 Percy Street
London W1P 0LD

First published in
the United States in 1996 by
Copper Beech Books
an imprint of
The Millbrook Press
2 Old New Milford Road
Brookfield
Connecticut 06804

Editor
Jim Pipe
Designed by
David West Children's Books
Designer
Simon Morse
Illustrated by
Mike Bell, Richard Berridge –
Specs Art,
Roger Hutchins
Additional illustrations by
David Burroughs
Rob Shone

Printed in Belgium
All rights reserved

Library of Congress Cataloging-
in-Publication Data

Finney, Fred, 1944-
Mystery history of a pirate
galleon / Fred Finney.
p. cm. — (Mystery history)
Includes index.
Summary: Describes life aboard a
pirate ship. Includes games,
puzzles, and mazes.
ISBN 0-7613-0496-7 (lib. bdg.).
— ISBN 0-7613-0502-5

Contents

Pirate Galleon

Hear the word "pirate," and you think of great galleons with murderous rogues swinging down from the rigging and guns blazing in a furious broadside. But pirates have been around for centuries – in 69 A.D. Roman general Julius Caesar was captured by Mediterranean pirates in galleys (*above*), and from the 8th century A.D., Viking longships terrorized the north European seas.

By 1650, when our story is set, galleons rule the waves. But even now, pirates prefer smaller boats suited to their tactics. Spanish galleons, however, *are* important to the pirates. Loaded with gold from the New World (see map *below*), they make a rich prize on their route home.

The Mystery of History

A few galleon wrecks have been brought up from the seabed, and there are some interesting accounts of pirate life written at the time. But these can only tell us part of the story. So as you read, try to imagine what life must have been like as a pirate. Who knows, your guess might be right. That's the real mystery of history!

THE SPANISH MAIN

Vera Cruz

Mexico

Cuba

Port Royal

Hispaniola

ATLANTIC OCEAN

CARIBBEAN SEA

PACIFIC OCEAN

Peru

You'll find that *Mystery History of a Pirate Galleon* is packed with puzzles and mysteries for you to solve. But before you go any further, read the instructions below to get the most out of the book!

Hunt the Rogue Pirate

One of the rascally crew has run off with the treasure! No one is sure who, but on page 29 a number of likely-looking rogues have been rounded up.

To help you work out which one of them is the greedy thief, six clues are given in the treasure hunt boxes (the panels with a treasure chest in the corner).

To get the right clues, however, you will need to answer the questions correctly – and that means reading the book carefully. Happy hunting!

Pirate Puzzles

The skull and crossbones marks a special puzzle that can be anything from a maze to a mathematical brainteaser. Answers are in The Scurvy Answers.

True or False

Some pages have a teasing True or False question with an answer (on page 29) that may surprise you!

I Spy Strangers

Spot the historical items hidden on some pages, then guess if they really belong in a 17th-century galleon!

History Mysteries

Dotted around the page are questions like: **Q1 Did big ships always have the advantage?** *Have a think about these before reading the answer in The Scurvy Answers.*

The Scurvy Answers

*Answers to I Spy Strangers 🔍, the History Mysteries **Q2**, and the Pirate Puzzles ☠ are given in this panel at the bottom of the page.*

Buried Treasure Game

At the back of the book are full answers to I Spy Strangers and True or False, a rogues, gallery of likely-looking villains (one of whom has made off with the treasure), and, last but not least, a great aerial view of an island that is also an exciting treasure hunt (right)!

The Spanish Main

Q1 Where does all the gold and silver come from?

On the dockside at Vera Cruz, Mexico, soldiers and slaves are loading gold and silver onto a huge Spanish galleon. The treasure will go to the King of Spain – unless pirates, hiding along the coast, grab it first.

Pirates are robbers of the seas. They attack ships and steal what they can – gold, jewels, goods, and even people, who can be held for ransom. The Spanish Main (the Spanish empire in the New World, see map on page 2) has been a favorite place for wicked sea dogs ever since Christopher Columbus reached America in 1492.

The Scurvy Answers

Q1 From the gold and silver mines of Mexico and Peru (see map on page 2), and from melted-down Aztec and Inca works of art. Many beautiful pieces are destroyed in this way. If they don't have time to melt them down, the greedy Spaniards crush the works of art so they can fit as many as possible into their large galleons. When Francisco Pizarro ransomed the Inca leader Atahualpa in 1533, the Inca people filled a room seven paces long and six paces wide with gold. Once he had the gold, Pizarro killed Atahualpa anyway.

Q2 He wasn't! He was really trying to reach China and India by sailing west. He knew the world was round but he thought it was smaller than it actually is. Right up to his death he believed that he had reached the East Indies and would not accept that he had discovered a new continent.

Q2 Why was Columbus looking for America?

Q3 Are pirates only a danger in the Caribbean?

☠ Pieces of Eight

Pirates mostly use Spanish coins. Some of these are made from melted-down Aztec works of art (*left*). A gold doubloon is worth eight escudos. An escudo is worth two silver "pieces of eight" (*right*). One "piece of eight" can be cut into eight pieces, each worth a réal. If you are a pirate captain, how many réals should you get for your gold doubloon (*left*)?

◉ *I Spy Strangers*
Spot the derrick crane, galley, parrot, and cigar? Which don't belong in the Spanish Main?

Q3 No! Pirates aren't fussy where they work – they go wherever there are ships to plunder. When business in the Spanish Main drops off, many pirates will sail east to the Indian Ocean, looking for ships carrying spices, silks, and jewels. They even set up a pirate kingdom based on the island of Madagascar. Meanwhile local pirates terrorize the western coastline of India. During the 17th century, Muslim pirates (later known as Corsairs) are also at work in the Mediterranean. Finally, there is a long pirate tradition in China – one rogue, Ching Yi, has a fleet of 1,800 ships!

☠ Pieces of Eight

One escudo is worth 16 réals, so a doubloon is 8 x 16 réals = 128 réals!
See page 28 for the reasons why.

◉ *I Spy Strangers Answer: The derrick crane and galley don't belong.*

The Treasure Ship

The mighty Spanish galleon is sailing north, waiting for fair winds to cross the ocean. She is one of the world's tallest and strongest ships. She can carry up to 200 men and 60 cannons, as well as plenty of treasure.

But danger lurks among the Caribbean islands. The Spanish fear that their galleons will be attacked and captured by privateers. The privateers of England, France, and Holland are enemies of Spain. For safety, the treasure ships cross the Atlantic in a group of nearly a hundred ships.

I Spy Strangers
Can you spot the book, toilet, deckchair, and pig? Which don't belong on a Spanish galleon?

Q1 Why do you think the Spanish like tall ships?

The Scurvy Answers

Q1 The Spanish galleon is built to ride high in the water, so that she can carry more soldiers and cargo and can get closer to shore. Her high decks also make it easier for soldiers to fight the enemy in close combat, as when two ships grapple with each other, the men on the taller ships have an advantage. However, big ships are easier to hit with cannonballs, and move and turn more slowly.

I Spy Strangers Answer: The deck chair and toilet don't belong. See page 28 for the reasons why.

Q2 Because England is Protestant and Spain is Catholic. At this time Catholics and Protestants were fighting all over Europe. The Spanish wanted to make England Catholic again. In 1588, they sent a huge Armada (fleet) to invade England, but it was destroyed by storms.

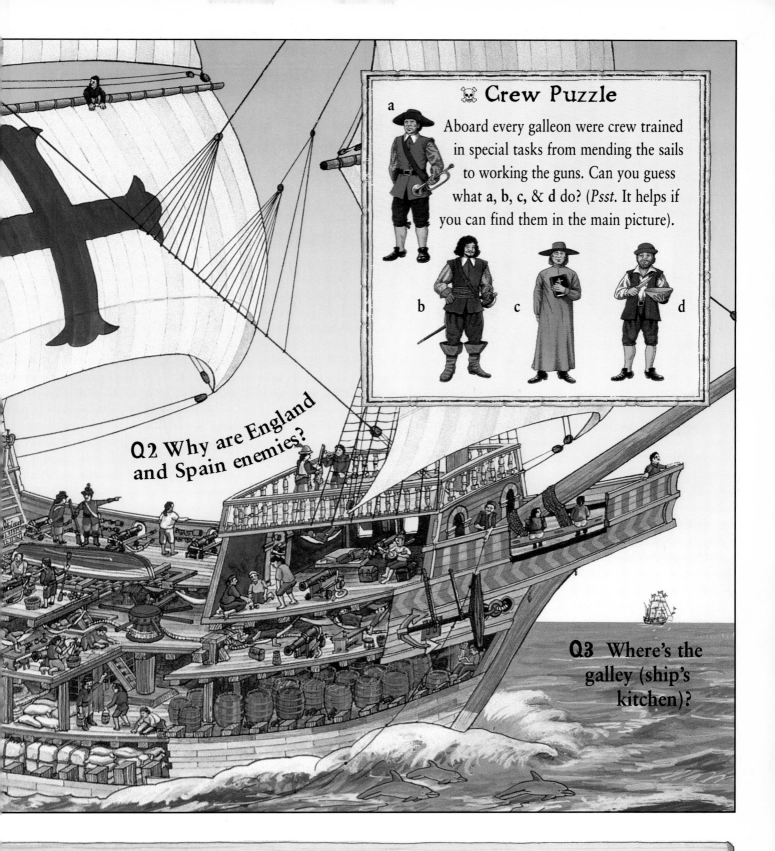

☠ Crew Puzzle

a Aboard every galleon were crew trained in special tasks from mending the sails to working the guns. Can you guess what **a**, **b**, **c**, & **d** do? (*Psst.* It helps if you can find them in the main picture).

b   c   d

Q2 Why are England and Spain enemies?

Q3 Where's the galley (ship's kitchen)?

Q3 There isn't one, and neither is there a cook! Amazingly, everyone prepares their own meals. The Spanish King supplies all sailors with food at his own expense, and everything they are given in their monthly ration – e.g. salty meat and onions – is raw. Many bring their own supplies on board.

A stove is set up near the main mast at eight or nine o'clock each morning and two sentries watch over it until it is put out at four o'clock. Imagine dozens of pots standing over the stove and the same number of people pushing and jostling each other for space around it – utter chaos!

☠ Crew Puzzle

a *The trumpeter (who sounds the captain's commands).* **b** *The pilot (who makes sure the ship is sailing in the right direction).* **c** *The priest.* **d** *The barber (who as well as cutting hair is in charge of curing the crew by draining their blood – see page 17).*

The Privateers

Even in peacetime, English naval commanders like Sir Francis Drake (c.1549–1596) and Sir John Hawkins (1532–1595) attacked Spanish ships and took home their treasure. Drake and Hawkins owned their ships, so they were called "privateers." They usually carried letters of marque (license) from the Queen which allowed them to attack Spanish ships but no others. The Spanish said they were just pirates.

Seventy years later, privateers are still hunting Spanish treasure ships. But how do they find their way around a huge ocean? Sailors who figure out the ship's position are called navigators. Pirates call them "sea artists." At best, a good sea artist can figure out a position at sea to within a mile, but on deck in a storm they make quick, rough judgments. Look lively, boys! Ship ahoy! They've spotted a lone galleon.

☠ Hidden Treasure

Follow the directions below (N = North etc.) to find Captain Kidd's real treasure chest. Your ship starts on square B9. If

1
2
3
4
5
6
7
8
9
10

you hit land or meet the Spanish fleet, you've gone wrong!

4   N – 4 squares
5   NE – 1 square
6   E – 3 squares
7   SE – 1 square
8   NE – 1 square
    N – 1 square
9   NW – 2 squares
10 E – 4 squares

A B C D E F G H I J

Q1 Why do seamen need to know where they are so quickly?

☠ Hidden Treasure

Captain Kidd actually buried his treasure on square J1! If you thought it was one of the other, false treasure chests, then try again and see where you went wrong!

The Scurvy Answers

Q1 They often need to get back to base as quickly as possible for fear of storms, enemy ships, and hunger. If they are pirates, they want to find the routes taken by the Spanish fleet.

Q2 Not always. It depends on how often sailors have sailed in the region before and how good their instruments really are.

To help voyagers, mapmakers divide the world into vertical segments (lines of longitude) and horizontal rings (lines of latitude).

Q2 Are the maps any good?

Q3 How do "sea artists" find out where they are?

True or False? Pirates only attack ships.

I Spy Strangers
Can you spot the compass, telescope, tea, radio, and wristwatch? Which don't belong on a privateer ship?

Q3 They look at the shoreline and the stars through a telescope. They are helped by charts and globes, and astronomical instruments called astrolabes and volvelles. They also use a backstaff to work out latitudes from the place of the sun in the sky. This is then checked against a set of tables.

You can tell where north is just by using the sun and a watch (preferably one that keeps time well!). You just point the hour hand at the sun.

Imagine a line bisecting the angle between the hour hand and 12 o'clock. This is south – so north is the opposite direction!

I Spy Strangers
Answer: the wristwatch and the radio. See page 28 for the full answers.

9

Battle at Sea

The English privateer has caught up with the lone galleon separated from the rest of the fleet. She has pulled alongside and is swapping broadsides with the Spanish ship. Cannonballs can put holes in the side of the enemy ship, or smash the masts and sails, making the boat impossible to sail.

The Spanish do not like this way of fighting. They prefer to board the enemy and use their soldiers in hand-to-hand fighting as on land. Sea battles can take several hours, with the fighting moving from one ship to the other.

> *I Spy Strangers*
> *Can you spot the longbow, fireworks, tennis racket, and plaster cast? Which don't belong in a 17th-century sea battle?*

Q1 Do big ships always have the advantage?

The Scurvy Answers

Q1 Not always. In the 16th century, English sailor John Hawkins built a new type of English galleon, lower in the water and faster than the great Spanish "sea castles." It also carries long-range cannons.

These ships allow the English sea captains to surprise the enemy and cause a lot of damage before the Spanish ships can make use of their many soldiers and high decks.

I Spy Strangers: The plaster cast and tennis racket don't belong. For the reasons why see page 28.

Q2 You must be joking! The swirling smoke from the guns, deafening noise, darkness below decks, and false flags make it all very confusing! Once hand-to-hand fighting starts, the only way officers can lead their men is to go first and hope that everyone else follows!

True or False?
Some pirates are
also slave traders.

Q2 Is it always clear
what's going on?

☠ **Life at Sea?**
What do you think is the
most dangerous aspect of life
at sea for 17th-century sailors?
☠ Drowning or being eaten
    by sharks (*top*)?
    ☠ Dying from disease (often
    spread by rats, *above*)?
☠ Dying of starvation (*left*)?
☠ Or being killed in
battle (*right*)?

Q3 Is it safe
being a gunner?

Q3 Not at all! The heavy guns, weighing hundreds of pounds, jump back when they are fired and often fly loose across the deck, smashing into anyone around. And if a cannon misfires, the exploding gunpowder sends deadly pieces of hot metal flying in their faces.

☠ **Life at Sea?**
In fact, more sailors die from disease than any other cause. Dirty conditions and often rotting food mean that once one sailor is infected, disease quickly spreads to the rest of the crew. Sailors do drown quite often, partly because most never learn how to swim. Sharks are naturally attracted by the scent of blood at any battle. Starvation is also a problem for pirates, who can't stock up on supplies as easily as a galleon. In any case, they did not take the best food, and rarely sailed with fruit or vegetables.

The Buccaneers

Q1 Where do the buccaneers come from?

Q2 How can a few buccaneers capture a galleon?

☠ The Barbecue Lovers

The buccaneers' name comes from the word "*boucan*," a smokehouse where hunters prepare meat from the cows they have caught. Why do you think they smoke meat?

☠ The Barbecue Lovers

Because the Caribbean islands are one of the last places they're likely to find snow or ice to keep meat fresh, the buccaneers have learned from the native Arawak tribes that the best way to "cure" (preserve) meat for as long as possible is to smoke it!

The Scurvy Answers

Q1 The buccaneers come from many different backgrounds – nearly all of them are men. Some are European farmers who have had their farms and crops destroyed by the Spanish. Others are escaped criminals or deserters from privateer ships.

There are also runaway slaves among the buccaneers. These men have been shipped to the Caribbean from Africa to work on the sugar and tobacco plantations. Despite their different backgrounds, many of the men form close friendships with each other.

A hundred miles further south, a murderous gang of cruel and dirty buccaneers are rushing to their boats to attack a Spanish galleon that has sailed into view. They lead a rough, lawless life and dress in smelly animal skins covered in blood.

The Spanish are trying to get rid of the buccaneers, who live on the rocky island of Hispaniola. But these wild men have ganged up to fight back by attacking Spanish ships. They have turned their long meat knife into a short sword called a cutlass. Many buccaneers are so good at capturing Spanish gold that they have stopped living off the island and are now full-time pirates.

Hunt the Rogue Pirate 1
What is a cutlass?

a Angry young woman = No hair
b Caribbean squid = Fair hair
c Short sword = Black hair

Get the right answer and you get a clue to the identity of the rogue pirate on page 29.

Q3 Do you think living as a hunter on a Caribbean island could be fun?

I Spy Strangers
Can you spot the satchel, life preserver, sneakers, and beach umbrella? Which don't belong on a buccaneer island?

Q2 By ganging up! By the mid-17th century so many buccaneers have ganged together they are known as the "Brethren of the Coast." When Henry Morgan asked for their help in 1668, 33 ships and 1,800 buccaneers came to join him.

Though they start off in smaller boats, many buccaneers adapt the larger boats they capture, forming a fleet that would terrify a squadron of Spanish treasure galleons.

Q3 Only if you had plenty of food and drink and the Spanish fleet aren't chasing after you!

I Spy Strangers Answer: the life preserver, sneakers, and beach umbrella don't belong. For the reasons why turn to page 28.

OLPH library

Who's in Charge?

The buccaneers have captured the ship and some of the Spanish crew have joined them. They are now trying to decide who should be captain. The old one was put ashore in Jamaica a month ago, because he was too cruel. Two of the toughest men are having a brawl to decide who will take over. Some blood has been shed, but it's not a fight to the death.

On a pirate ship, power lies with the crew rather than the captain. If the crew find a person guilty (even the captain), they can take a vote on it and get rid of him. Pirates vote on what the rules should be.

Women and gambling are banned because they lead to trouble. Every man must fight hard in battle and keep his weapons ready for fighting. If he doesn't, he will be killed by his fellow pirates. Fighting on board ship is forbidden, and all arguments are settled by duels on land.

Q1 Do women ever become pirates?

◉ I Spy Strangers
Can you spot the woman, sunglasses, violin, cabin boy, and clothespin? Which of these don't belong on a buccaneer ship?

The Scurvy Answers

Q1 Not usually. A few daring women go to sea dressed up as men! Two of the most famous are Anne Bonny (d. 1720) who joined pirate "Calico Jack" Rackham when she fell in love with him, and Mary Read (1690–1720). When a fellow pirate insulted her lover, Read challenged him to a duel. Minutes later, she had run her male opponent through with a cutlass.

Q2 You can be voted captain by the crew, as Welshman Bartholemew Roberts was in 1719. The crew want someone who can keep order and take decisions. A captain has to be tough, fair, and clever if he is to stay in the job. But however good he is, in the end he must answer to the crew!

◉ *I Spy Strangers Answer: All but the violin don't belong! For the reasons why turn to page 28.*

Q2 How can you become a captain?

Q3 What type of people become pirates?

*True or false?
All booty was
divided out equally.*

☠ The Pirate Code

Some pirates wrote down their rules. Look at the list below and see if you can spot which two rules were *not* among those set down by pirate Captain John Phillips:

a Everyone may have a share of captured drink and fresh food.

b Gambling with cards (*above*) is forbidden.

c Musicians have only one day off a week.

d The compensation for losing an arm or leg is 800 silver dollars.

e Anyone being lazy will lose his share of the booty.

f The captain's word is final.

g Anyone found stealing will have his ears and nose slit open.

h Lights out at 8:00 p.m.

Q3 Pirates can be people who are captured ashore and forced to go to sea (press-ganged); seamen or slaves who have run away from other ships, or just those who like adventure or are greedy for wealth.

☠ **The Pirate Code**
Rules f and b have been made up. The captain's word was never final and rough pirates went to bed when they liked. The others are part of the real pirate code.

All Hands on Deck

Q1 How do pirates measure the time?

True or false? Pirates made their captives walk the plank.

The new captain has to make sure everyone works hard to keep the ship working well. He is helped by a number of officers: the pilot charts the right course for the ship; the master gives the orders to the rest of the crew; the boatswain is in charge of setting the sails; and the steward looks after the ship's stores.

The ship needs plenty of craftsmen: a carpenter; a caulker who fixes the ship's hull with tar; and a cook to prepare the ghastly food. Big ships have gunners. The seamen are split into two teams. One team works for four hours at a time (a watch), while the other team rests; then the two teams change places. But in a storm, no one gets much sleep!

> 🔍 *I Spy Strangers*
> *Can you spot the turtle, flashlight, sleeping bag, and wooden leg? Which of these don't belong on a buccaneer ship?*

The Scurvy Answers

Q1 With an hour glass. It takes half an hour for the sand to pass through. Eight turns of the hour glass make up a "watch" at sea. After each turn of the glass the bell is rung – one chime after half an hour and two chimes after an hour. At the end of the watch eight chimes are rung, and someone might cry: "Eight bells and all's well!" Did you spot the hourglass on the galleon on page 6?

I Spy Strangers Answer: The flashlight and sleeping bag don't belong! For the reasons why, *turn to page 28.*

Q2 The crew have to: clean weapons so that they can fight well; mend sails, spars, and ropes so the boat sails well; scrub the deck so the worms don't eat away the planks; and pump the bilges so that the boat doesn't sink from being full of water.

Q2 What jobs must the crew do?

Hunt the Rogue Pirate 2

Which sea do the Corsair pirates sail in?

a Mediterranean = Green pants

b Red Sea = Red pants

c Caribbean Sea = Brown/gray pants

Use your clue to figure out who the rogue buccaneer is on page 29.

Bilge pump

Stores of spare sails and rigging

Stones to keep ship upright

Q3 Is there a fast way to figure out a boat's speed?

Q3 Yes. Drop a float into the sea at the bow of the boat and see how long it takes to reach the stern (like the man on page 7). Your speed is equal to the length of the boat divided by the time it takes the float to come past.

☠ **Medical Puzzle** The record for removing a leg before the use of anesthetics (drugs that knock you out) is 33 seconds. But the doctor was in such a hurry he accidentally cut three fingers off his assistant's hand.

☠ Medical Puzzle

Medicine aboard ship is crude. The cure for anything from malaria to dysentery is the removal of "bad" blood (done by the barber, *below*). Surgery is performed as quickly as possible to keep wounds from going bad. The only way to stop the terrible pain is to make patients drunk. How long do you think it takes to saw off an injured leg?

These pirates are sitting down to a meal, and trying to make the best of it. Life at sea is tough for everybody. Unless the pirates get some fresh fish or meat, such as tuna or wild birds, the food is revolting. One standard item is hardtack, a tough cookie made out of flour and water. This often gets full of weevils (see picture in Watery Grave puzzle on page 11)!

Without fresh fruit or vegetables, the crew will soon get ill. Sickness is common because of the poor diet and crowded spaces. The water is undrinkable so pirates have good reason to make sure they bring plenty of beer and wine.

Q1 What is scurvy and why do so many seamen die of it?

Q2 Which creatures usually eat well on ships?

Q3 What are weevils?

☠ What's For Dinner?

At sea for long periods, pirates were forced to eat what was available. Which of the following foods do you think formed part of their regular diet?

Fish

Turtles

Beef & milk

Eggs

Snakes

Each other

☠ What's For Dinner?

Fish, eggs (laid by chickens kept on board), and turtles (kept alive in the hold until needed) were often on the menu. There was no milk or fresh beef, only meat that had been salted. When their other food ran out, pirates turned to more bizarre sources – on one island all they could find were snakes and monkeys! And yes, on very rare occasions they did end up eating each other.

Hunt the Rogue Pirate 3

How do you catch scurvy?

a   By eating too much Vitamin C
    = Eye patch

b   By not eating enough fresh fruit
    = Wooden leg

c   By wearing dirty underwear
    = No eye patch or wooden leg

Use the clue to find the rogue pirate.

🔍 **I Spy Strangers**
Spot the fruit, playing cards, mousetrap, false teeth, and teddy bear. Which don't belong on a buccaneer ship ?

The Scurvy Answers

Q1 Scurvy is a disease caused by the lack of vitamin C (available only in fresh fruit and vegetables). What does it feel like? Your gums hurt, boils erupt under your skin, your arms and legs ache, your hair falls out, and then you probably die.

So make sure you eat your vegetables every day! Without regular supplies of fruit and vegetables, pirates often caught the disease.

Q2 Rats (can you see one?) eat through the food, ropes, and wood; worms eat through the ship's sides; and weevils take the cookies – just

about everything on board can be eaten except the sailors!

Q3 Beetle larvae, the grubs that eat the grub!

🔍 I Spy Strangers Answer: The teddy bear, playing cards, and fresh fruit don't belong! For the reasons why turn to page 28.

Wine, Women, & Song

Here the buccaneers are having a wild time at an inn. Now they can do all the things they're not allowed to do on ship. Port Royal, on the island of Jamaica, is their favorite place.

If they've got plenty of booty, many pirates spend it here on alcohol, gambling, and women. Drunken pirates often get into fights and have all their money stolen. Rum, made from Jamaican sugarcane, is a favorite drink. Some pirates also have to work on shore, careening or fixing (see page 21) their boats.

Life was one long party at Port Royal until one day in 1692. An earthquake created a tidal wave which destroyed the town completely.

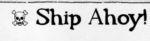

Hunt the Rogue Pirate 4
Where is Port Royal?

a On the buccaneer island of Hispaniola = Green jacket

b The Royal Docks in London = No jacket

c On Jamaica = Red jacket

Your clue will help you to find the rogue pirate on page 29.

☠ Ship Ahoy!

a

b

c

If you were the captain of a Spanish galleon, you'd keep one of your crew high up in the crow's nest to keep a close eye on the horizon for any sign of danger.

However, it wasn't always easy to tell whether a ship was friendly or not. Can you tell which ships on the *right* should be avoided? (*Psst*. It might help to look at other ships in the book).

☠ Ship Ahoy!

The number of masts gives you a clue. a is a small galleon (3 masts) and could belong to privateers, b (1 mast) could be a buccaneer boat, while c is a large galleon (4 masts), so is probably not a pirate ship.

Scurvy Answers

Q1 A tidal wave, or tsunami, is a huge wave caused by an earthquake. When the earth changes shape, the sea bed also shifts. The waves don't seem big out at sea, but once they come into shallower water they can reach heights of 100 ft or more. Other huge tsunami have destroyed towns at Kalliste in the Mediterranean and on Java and Sumatra in the Pacific.

Q2 Carouse (which means to drink lots of alcohol noisily) – definitely. Though it has to be done, careening is too much like hard work.

Q1 What are tidal waves?

Q2 Do pirates prefer to careen or carouse?

True or False?
The pirate Blackbeard used to drink a mixture of rum and gunpowder.

The Jolly Sailor

📷 *I Spy Strangers*
Spot the matches, saxophone, camera, and bikini. Which don't belong at Port Royal?

☠ On the Beach

Pirates depend on speed for success. To ensure this they regularly clean (careen) the bottom of their ship. The ship is dragged out of the water and tipped on its side. The men scrape off all the seaweed and barnacles (*above*) with chisels (*right*). What other repairs do you think were carried out while the ship was on the beach?

☠ On the Beach
The most important repair was caulking, or making sure the ship was watertight. The seams between the planks were stripped, filled with unraveled rope, and sealed with hot pitch (tar). Repairs to sails and other parts of the boat could usually be carried out at sea.

📷 *I Spy Strangers Answer: None of them belong!*
For the reasons why, turn to page 29.

Pirate Attack!

It is evening. The light is beginning to fade, and the buccaneer ship slips out of the bay like a ghost. As it moves in to attack the Spanish treasure ship, no cannons are fired – the buccaneers are hoping to catch the bigger ship by surprise. They know their small ship is too small to win in a battle of the broadsides with the great galleon.

The buccaneers have thrown the grappling irons up onto the deck of the bigger boat and are pulling alongside. The men are swarming aboard. They're armed to the teeth with cutlasses, pistols, and muskets. The galleon's rudder is jammed so it cannot escape.

There are too many buccaneers and they fight too fiercely for the frightened Spaniards. Soon the Spanish captain is surrounded and the fight is over. The ship is taken.

Q1 How would you sneak up on a big ship?

◉ *I Spy Strangers*
Can you spot the suit of armor, blowpipe, balaclava, frogman, and mobile phone. Which don't belong in a pirate galleon?

The Scurvy Answers

Q1 Quietly, perhaps at night. Keep out of the line of the big guns at the side. Then climb aboard and cut down the sails and rigging. At the last moment, let out bloodcurdling screams to terrify your victims. Some pirates carry a group of musicians, known as a pirate orchestra, to make terrifying noises on their instruments.

Q2 Yes. They sometimes fly the flag of a friendly nation, or hide their guns. Some crews are said to dress up as women. Since pirate ships don't carry women, the victims think they are safe.

Q3 When you need to keep your weapons hidden, and when you're fighting in closed spaces belowdecks. The cutlass of the buccaneers – longer than a dagger but shorter than a sword – is a good halfway solution.

◉ *I Spy Strangers Answer: None of the items belong! See page 29.*

Q2 Do pirates use dirty tricks?

Hunt the Rogue Pirate 5

What are barnacles?

a A horrible disease = No shoes

b An animal that clings to the bottom of ships = Sea boots

c A type of handcuffs = Black shoes

One of the buccaneers has stolen the treasure. Get the right answer and use the clue to find out who it is.

Q3 When is a dagger often better than a sword?

☠ Hoist the Jolly Roger

The pirate flag – the Jolly Roger – warned their victims to give up without a fight. But which two of these flags (*below*) aren't real?

A

B

C

D

E

F

☠ The Jolly Roger

D isn't a real pirate flag as revolvers weren't invented until two hundred years later. E isn't because pirates wouldn't show a skeleton playing soccer! The black and white flag became popular at the end of the 17th century. The original Jolly Roger was in fact red – B belongs to Christopher Moody. A belongs to Jack Rackham, C belongs to Blackbeard, and flag F is flown by Captain Dulaïen.

Dividing the Booty

Q1 Can you get rich from piracy?

The Scurvy Answers

Q1 Sometimes. A share of a big treasure ship is huge! When Thomas Tew raided a ship in the Indian Ocean in 1693, every member of the crew received a share that would be worth millions of dollars today. However, such enormous prizes are very rare and pirate crews usually divide up much more modest treasures.

Q2 It depends on who captures you. The cruelty of the buccaneers is legendary. On one occasion, Captain Francis L'Ollonais cut out the heart of one prisoner and stuffed it into the mouth of another. In 1668, Henry Morgan forced the men of the Cuban town of El Puerto del Principe to surrender by threatening to cut their wives and children to pieces. However, some pirates deliberately spread stories of their cruelty to encourage crews to surrender to them without a fight.

The pirates give a great cheer and immediately search the ship for everything they can find. They're in luck! The galleon is bursting with valuable cargo. The buccaneers will divide up the shares when they get ashore. What's more, they now have a huge sailing ship, which will serve as the flagship for the new buccaneer fleet.

The officers are questioned by the buccaneers about other Spanish ships. One tries to fight back but is caught and thrown overboard. Terrified Spanish sailors are locked away below decks. Many are praying for their lives. What will happen to them? They have heard terrible stories about pirate tortures.

True or False? Pirates never stay rich.

Q2 What do pirates do with their captives?

☠ Blag the Booty

Aboard the captured galleon the pirates are looking for all sorts of booty. They've brought everything up on deck to figure out what they want. Once you've spotted all the different items on deck in *I Spy Strangers*, can you guess which of them the pirates are going to take? *Psst.* A sugar loaf (*right*) is a cone of melted sugar poured into a mold for easy loading.

☠ Blag the Booty

Though pirates always hope to find a galleon loaded with gold, or jewelry, often they make do with smaller prizes. Just about everything has some use. Spare equipment, such as anchors, sails, ropes, and weapons are always needed, as are charts (some of which are very rare). Pirates also rely on stealing food, drink, and medicines (which are very rare and expensive). Sugar loaves are the one exception – though a luxury item in the 17th century, they are usually too bulky to take.

A Pirate's Fate

Marooned Pirates who break the ship's code are marooned – put on a lonely island and left with a few supplies to live on.

Get Rich Quick Some pirates do strike it lucky, such as the crew of Captain Henry Avery, who each made $1,000 after the capture of the Arab ship *Gang-i-Sawai*.

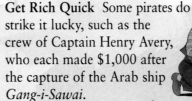

Go to Jail
In fact, few pirates are ever caught. Even when they are found guilty, many escape execution and are pardoned after spending time in jail. By the 18th century, some prisons are ships.

Die in Battle
A pirate captain expects to lose several of his crew every time they attack a ship. And once pirates begin to loot shipping from every country and not just Spanish galleons, they risk having to fight off navy ships wherever they sail.

Starve to Death
Starvation is a real fear among pirates. When food runs out and no port is safe to enter, there is little they can do except pray for a victim to turn up.

Become Captain
An ambitious and brave pirate may get voted captain by the rest of the crew. Like Sir Henry Morgan, he might even get a pardon and a knighthood for attacking the Spanish!

☠ Your Fate Maze (above)
A pirate's life was one of chance. You could either strike it lucky or find yourself at the end of the hangman's rope. Starting at the center, find your way out of the maze above and see what fate has in store for you – there are six possible solutions!

The Scurvy Answers
Q1 Not every time. When Captain William Kidd was sent to the gallows in 1701, a large crowd gathered to watch the grisly spectacle. But when the trapdoor opened, the rope snapped. However, unfortunately for Kidd, it worked on the second attempt. His dead body was then chained to a post to be washed by the tide three times.

Finally, the corpse was covered in tar (to make it last) and hung in an iron cage from a gibbet beside the Thames River, in London, England, where passing seamen could see it.

Pirates punish their prisoners in different ways. Some are flogged with a-cat-o'-nine tails, a maritime whip with knots at the end. Many of the men are to be marooned on a desert island – they will be lucky to survive. Important captives are ransomed, and some seamen will be sold or used as slaves. Most pirates live short but exciting lives. They know that if they are caught they may be hanged, perhaps at London's famous Execution Dock. Hanging is the traditional punishment for pirates. Their bodies are often left to hang for several days as a warning to others not to repeat their crimes – but few pirates will ever come to London.

Hunt the Rogue Pirate 6

Where do the buccaneers get their name from?

a A type of wild horse = Hat

b A French word for piracy = Scarf

c A method of preserving meat = No headgear

Now you have all six clues, turn to page 29 and identify the rogue pirate.

Q2 Did piracy end with the buccaneers?

I Spy Strangers
Spot the scissors, steamboat, toga, and newspaper? Which don't belong in the 17th century?

Q2 Not at all. Pirates are still operating not just in the Caribbean but in many parts in the world. The parrots and the wooden legs are gone, but the tactics remain the same – speed, terror, and surprise. Modern pirates use small but very fast power boats that shoot out from hidden bays, then threaten their victims with guns and rockets. There are few gold-carrying galleons around today, but the pirates earn a good living from stealing electrical items like computers, watches, and T.V.s. They work quickly and communicate with mobile phones so it is very hard for naval patrols to catch them. In 1991, there were 150 pirate attacks in Indonesian waters alone.

I Spy Strangers Answer: The steamship and the toga don't belong. For the reasons why turn to page 29.

I Spy Strangers

Pages 4–5

Legend has it that Archimedes (287–212 B.C.) used a *crane* to pull the ships of his Roman enemies out of the water! But until the 18th century, cranes were powered by animals or humans. *Galleys* (boats powered by oars) were invented around 2000 B.C., but by the 16th century they were only used by Mediterranean pirates. A more common sight was the galleas, a ship powered by sails and oars (*top*). *Parrot*s are common in tropical areas, though some species are disappearing because they are popular as pets. Natives of Cuba were already smoking *cigars* before Columbus arrived in 1492.

Pages 6–7

Books were a great luxury but a sailor might carry one of the new, cheap bibles. Live animals were often carried on board as food – *pigs* were taken to the Caribbean by the Spanish. Sir John Harington invented a *toilet* for Queen Elizabeth I in 1589, but toilets didn't catch on until the 1700s when plumbing and sewage had greatly improved. *Deck chairs* were first used on ships in the 19th century.

Pages 8–9

By 80 A.D. the Chinese had devised a kind of turning magnetic needle, and the *compass* was used in Europe by 12th century. The *telescope* was first invented by Dutchman Hans Lippershey in 1608. The Dutch brought *tea* back from China in 1609, but it didn't catch on until 1660 – so the captain is very fashionable. *Radios* weren't available until Guglielmo Marconi invented them in 1895 – not even for pirate stations! The *watch* was invented around the year 1500 (*above*), but the first *wrist*watch didn't appear until 1790.

Pages 10–11

The *bow and arrow* was largely replaced by pistols and muskets, but they were still used for firing bombs onto enemy decks. *Tennis* was first developed in France in the 1200s but it's unlikely that anyone used a racket in a sea battle! The *plaster cast* was first used to heal broken bones in 18th-century Iran. *Fireworks* were first invented by the Chinese in c.1100 A.D. English sea captains used them to set fire to enemy galleons.

Pages 12–13

In 1670, Captain Morgan's buccaneers were so hungry that they roasted their *satchels* and ate them! The first *life preserver* was made out of cork by Napoleon E. Overin of New York who obtained a patent in 1841, so the best thing you could throw to a drowning buccaneer was a piece of wood or an inflated pig's bladder. The *sneaker* – an early training shoe made of canvas with a rubber sole – was not dreamed up until 1927. Pirates had to make do with leather shoes or bare feet. The *umbrella* goes back to King Sargon of Akkad who used one around 2400 B.C., but buccaneers would have just stretched a piece of canvas on a frame of sticks for protection.

Pages 14–15

The *violin* was perfected by the late 17th century. Most ships had a fiddler who played tunes to help the sailors work. *Women* and *boys* were forbidden on pirate ships as they were believed to lead to trouble among the crew, but a few women did manage to go to sea as pirates, dressed up as men (see page 14). *Clothes pins* weren't invented until 1849 so they weren't even used for clothes in buccaneer times, let alone earrings! *Sunglasses* were first made in the United States in 1895 from tinted window glass, so there were no cool shades for the buccaneers to wear.

Pages 16–17

Turtles were carried live on boats as a source of fresh food. The first *electric flashlight* was developed in England in 1891. Anyone could make a *sleeping bag* by sewing up animal skins, but no pirate would have had a *zipper*, which wasn't invented until 1914. The first *wooden leg* seems to have been worn by an Athenian called Hegistratus who was captured by the Spartans in 479 B.C. He sawed off his foot to escape and got someone to make him a wooden replacement! In the early 16th century, Ambroise Paré, a French barber, came up with the first artificial hands — one of these had little cogs and pulleys to move the fingers (*above left*).

Pages 18–19

Teddy bears only became popular early in the 20th century when President Theodore "Teddy" Roosevelt made himself popular with the voters by

Hunt the Rogue Pirate
Now's the time to use your six clues to work out which of these shifty-looking buccaneers (right) has hidden the treasure away for himself. Perhaps you saw one of them doing something suspicious on pages 12–25? If you can't tell who the rogue pirate is from your clues, some of your answers must be wrong. The answer is given on page 32!

refusing to shoot a trapped bear. In any case, pirates were much too tough to want teddy bears. The first *false teeth* seem to have been developed by the Etruscans in Italy in about 700 B.C. but were too expensive for most pirates. No one took *fresh fruit* on long journeys until Captain Cook in the 18th century. *Mousetraps* with springs have been in use since the 13th century, though lots of other traps have been designed (*top*). *Playing cards* were invented in 10th-century China as a form of paper dice, and reached Europe in the 14th century. But pirates were not allowed to gamble on board ship!

Pages 20–21

Bikinis were worn in Roman times (*left*), but they were reinvented by French designer Louis Reard in 1946. An atomic bomb had just been tested at Bikini atoll in the Pacific. *Matches* were discovered accidentally in 1826 by John Walker, an English druggist. He was trying to find a chemical that would catch fire easily in a gun. When he tried to wipe the chemical off the end of a stick by rubbing it on the ground, it caught fire! The *saxophone* didn't appear until Adolphe Sax, a Belgian, patented it in 1846. The first photograph was taken by Joseph Niepce in France in 1826 and 13 years later *cameras* were sold in stores.

Pages 22–23

Once guns were invented, *armor* didn't offer much protection. Pirates could well have come across *blowpipes* in the New World but they wouldn't have been much use in a sea battle. A *balaclava* is a knitted hat that partly covers the face. It was worn by soldiers to protect themselves from the bitter cold. Balaclava was the place where in 1854 Lord Cardigan led the disastrous Charge of the Light Brigade. *Wet suits* are a 20th-century invention, although Aristotle mentions a diving bell in ancient Greek times. The first useful *diving suit* was not made until 1715. *Mobile phones* are a 20th-century invention!

Pages 26–27

The first useful *steamboat* (*above*) was built by the Claude Jouffrey d'Abbans in France in 1783. She was a 138 ft-long paddleboat, and she was the first boat ever to move against the current under her own power. *Scissors* were first used by the ancient Egyptians over three thousand years ago. They looked like tongs with knives instead of spoons on the end. The *toga* died out with the Roman empire and has only been worn since at wild parties! *Newspapers* were first printed in the early 17th century.

True or False

Page 9 False – Pirates often raided ports as well.
Page 11 True – Privateer John Hawkins was one of the first people to ship slaves from Africa to America.
Page 15 False – Captains got *at least* 1½ times as much as the rest of the crew. Other officers, the master carpenter, boatswain, and gunner got 1¼ times as much, while cooks and others who didn't fight got less than everyone else.
Page 16 False – There is no evidence that any pirates ever drowned their captives by making them walk the plank.
Page 21 True – Or so the stories say!
Page 25 False – Though some pirates blew their money, a few hid their wealth, collected it later and became respectable citizens.

Play the Game
Once you have picked out the rogue pirate, try to track down his buried treasure on pages 30–31.

Bloodbath Jack   Barnacle Bob   Mad Dog Roberts   Nathaniel Teach   One-eye Jarvis   Yellowbeard Bill   Crusher Sharp   Pete the Peg   Cutthroat Carlos

Treasure Hunt Rules

The rogue pirate has hidden the treasure in one of eleven places around the pirate island. To find out where, get the correct answer to each puzzle and write down the letter it gives you.

When you have all eleven letters, try rearranging them until you have spelled one of the places on the island. For example, if the letters you get are: S, L, C, V, U, T, A, S, C, O, and E, then rearranged they make the answer **CUTLASS COVE**. The real answer is at the bottom of page 32. To get you started, here's one letter – "A"!

☠ Mix and Match

Yellowbeard Bill always cheats at cards. Below are some of the cards he has copied to help him cheat. However, only one is exactly like the original card. Choose the matching card to earn an easy second letter!

Original   K   D   S

CUTLASS COVE

RED MOUNTAIN

☠ Missing Pieces

Two vital pieces are missing from this map. One marks the treasure, the other shows a route through the reef. Remember to write down your letters!

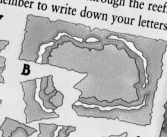

SNAKE FOREST

WHITE WATERS

SINKING SAND

☠ Weapon Watch

No pirate leaves home without a weapon in his hand. How many different weapons can you find in this book? Are there:

1   Between 0 and 5 = **O**
2   Between 5 and 10 = **R**
3   Between 10 and 15 = **N**

PISTOL POINT

☠ Mirror, Mirror

Look at this clue upside down in the mirror to get another letter:

Willor Willor on the wall, to tell is what I want. Cutlass; spells made following the Cutlass Captain Cobo, followed and Yellowbeard. Cutlass Chart and Cups – just not in Coconut

30

☠ DEADLY SWAMP MAZE

You are caught in the middle of the deadly swamp. Time is running out and you must escape before nightfall, when the crocodiles will be at their hungriest. Which of the three routes will be quickest? The shortest one gives you the right letter.

I C H

Exit

DEADLY SWAMP

TOTOC TEMPLE

GOLDEN FALLS

DEAD MAN'S BAY

SHARK ISLAND

☠ PIRATES OF THE WORLD

Match the pirates with their ships. If you think 1Δ-2Θ-3Φ is right, your letter is **M**, if you think 1Φ-2Θ-3Δ is right, your letter is **D**, and if you think 1Φ-2Δ-3Θ is right, your letter is **L**!

1

2

3

Δ

Φ

Θ

☠ MONKEY BUSINESS

On one ship in this book a cheeky monkey is clambering around in the rigging. Which ship is it?

1 Buccaneer Ship = **P**
2 Spanish Galleon = **S**
3 Privateer Ship = **L**

☠ ANIMAL LOOKOUT

How many different animals (land, sea, and air) can you find in the book? Are there:

1 Between 0 and 10 = **W & P**
2 Between 10 and 20 = **H & K**
3 Between 20 and 30 = **T & I**

This time the right answer gives you two letters for the price of one!

The Index

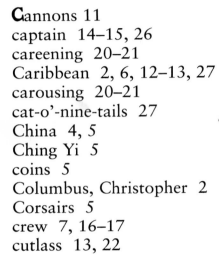

Hunt the Rogue Pirate
Ye Gad Sire, it was Mad
Dog Roberts all along
(left)! Did you see Mad
Dog dragging away the
heavy treasure chest on
page 21?

TREASURE! (look in mirror)
The answers are
(clockwise from the top)
SIDH☉KLAAKNS
. A letter, the skull and
crossbones, a cutlass
and a shark. Jumble them up and you
get: SHARK ISLAND! :g61